groovy chick's

guide to shopping and style

First published in Great Britain by HarperCollins Publishers Ltd in 2003

1 3 5 7 9 10 8 6 4 2

0-00-715221-3

Bang on the door character copyright:
Exclusive right to license by Santoro

www.bangonthedoor.com

Text © 2003 HarperCollins Publishers Ltd.

A CIP catalogue record for this title is available from the British Library.
The HarperCollins website address is: www.harpercollins.co.uk
Printed and bound in Hong Kong

bang on the door™ ©

groovy chick's

guide to shopping and style

Wanna be a groovy

chick just like me?

My groovy guide is full
of shopping and style
tips which will
transform you
into the grooviest
chick around.
So get ready to
sparkle and shine
from top to toe.

what's inside

how groovy

1 You're going to the school party.

What do you wear?

a) the lovely jumper grandma knitted for you

b) jeans and a shimmery top

c) your shiniest, glitziest party dress

2 You are going to the cinema. Which of these would you choose?

a) a t-shirt and your baggy old joggers

b) comfy combats, and cute trainers

c) your best sparkly jeans

3 You have £10 to spend in the sales. Which of these would you get?

a) an orange and green striped top

b) a cool denim backpack

c) glitter body gel

are you?

4 Your best mate calls and asks you to come round. Your hair's a mess. **What do you do?**

a) leave it
b) give it a brush and add some cute clips
c) spend ages washing and styling it

5 Your fave jeans have shrunk in the wash. **What do you do?**

a) wear them anyway
b) turn them into a cool cropped style
c) sew some shiny sequins round the bottom

6 Which of these shoes would you rather have?

a) another pair the same as the ones you have
b) the latest funky trainers
c) glittery party sandals

7 Yippee! It's time to choose the family holiday. Where would you go?

a) nowhere too far away
b) somewhere warm and sunny
c) star-studded Hollywood

8 If you could buy anything you liked in the whole world, what would it be?

a) a big house and your own pony
b) a cool 'n' cute car
c) a diamond tiara

FASHION FACT

During the 16th and 17th centuries shoes in Europe always had red heels.

Turn the page to discover your groovy chick grooviness rating

9

groovy chick's
grooviness ratings

Mostly As

Fashion disaster! Trying to get a cool look is just too much trouble, right? Wrong! Follow my simple style tips and you'll soon be a Groovy Chick like me.

Mostly Bs

Fashion fantastic! You are a pretty Groovy Chick and you just love to shop. My style guide will give you the best shopping ideas ever. Go girl!

Mostly Cs

Wow! You just love to sparkle and shine, but not every day's a disco. Sometimes less is more. I've got lots of ideas to help you get every look just right.

FASHION FACT

Fashion went wild in the 1960s. Crazy patterns and colours were mega popular and disposable paper clothes went on sale.

top 10
fashion do's and don'ts

1 Cropped trousers show off pretty ankles.

2 Bootcut trouser styles make legs look longer.

3 Pink and red clash horribly.

4 Knee length skirts are most flattering.

5 Don't wear lots of patterns at the same time.

6 An outfit that's all one colour makes you look taller.

7 Vertical stripes will make you look taller. Horizontal stripes work the opposite way.

8 Bright colours look really great as long as you don't try to wear them all at once.

9 Make sure your shoes match your outfit.

10 Make sure everything fits!

beauty basics

Follow my simple steps and you'll soon have glowing skin, shiny hair and the nicest nails.

The easiest way to looking good is to make sure you eat lots of fruit and veg. The vitamins they contain are great for your skin, hair and nails.

Keep sweets, crisps and burgers for special treats and munch on things like carrot sticks and yogurt.

Get some exercise!

Exercise makes you fitter and you'll also feel happier, so get striding around the shops.

Wanna be fit and be cool? Get skipping! It's not just for kids, skipping is the funky new fitness craze. The faster you skip, the fitter you'll get.

Phew!

12

To keep your skin looking great wash morning and night and rinse well. Smooth on a little light moisturiser.

For shiny, happy hair use a little conditioner every time you wash. Heated stylers can also damage and dry out your hair, so try not to use them too much.

Keep nails neat and sweet filing in one direction from the side towards the centre. Protect them with a coat of clear polish. No biting allowed.

Finally, don't forget to smile. Happy faces are so much prettier than frowny ones.

13

beauty busters

Here's how to sort out those spots, banish bad hair and get groovy.

Got a spot? Put a little toothpaste on it before going to bed. The toothpaste will help dry the spot as you sleep.

A little petroleum jelly from the chemist smeared on to your eyelashes will make them look longer and keep them in tip top condition.

If you have longish hair try plaiting it into four braids while it's wet and leave it to dry naturally. When you take them out you'll have lovely soft waves.

make a fruity facepack

Mash a banana together with a teaspoon of runny honey and a dessertspoon of double cream. Smooth on, leave for 10 minutes and rinse off thoroughly.

14

Love swimming?

Wetting your hair and applying a little conditioner before you go in the pool will help stop chlorine damaging your lovely locks.

Always keep lip balm handy. The delicate skin on lips is very easily damaged by the weather.

Soothe sore and tired eyes with used teabags. Let them cool, pop them over your closed eyes and relax for 10 minutes.

FASHION FACT

Got a spot? In ancient times you would have used a paste made from butter and barley flour to cure it.

15

rainbow girl

The right colours can make you look oh–so–fabulous!
Warm or Cool?
Our skin tones are described as warm or cool. It's easy to find out which group you are in, all you need is two pieces of card — one bright pink and one bright orange.

Hold the cards at each side of your face and look into a mirror. If the PINK card is more flattering it will brighten and even out your skin tone and you are COOL.
If the ORANGE is more flattering you are WARM.

COOL Combinations

Hair — very pale blonde, dark blonde, brown, dark brown or black
Skin — light milky white, rosy, olive or dark tones
Eyes — blue, grey, blue green or dark brown

WARM Combinations

Hair — golden, strawberry blonde, copper, chestnut or dark brown with red or golden tones
Skin — cream, peachy, bronze or with golden tones
Eyes — green, blue green, deep blue, hazel or brown

16

Now just pick from your list.

Colours for COOL

White
Sugar pink
Baby blue
Lilac
Purple
Cherry red
Silver
Aqua

Colours for WARM

Cream or ivory
Rose pink
Powder blue
Scarlet
Peach
Gold
Chocolate
Mauve

Colour can also affect the way we feel.

GREEN will boost your brainpower and give you inspiration.

BLUE is the most relaxing chill out colour.

RED is an action colour, full of fire and get up 'n' go.

YELLOW will fill you with happiness.

PINK is sweet and girly. It's also calming.

ORANGE is the colour to cheer you up and give you energy.

PURPLE will calm your mind and clear your head.

FASHION FACTS

For hundreds of years fashion and colour have been connected.

Red dye was first produced by the Aztecs in Mexico. They crushed beetles called cochineals to get the colour.

Before the 1920s pink was considered a boy's colour!

Purple was very hard to get, so it became the colour of royalty. Snails were soaked in water to get the purple dye.

In ancient Rome, yellow was the favourite colour for weddings.

Brides in China and India wear red and gold. White is the colour of mourning in China.

Green is a calming colour. Lots of hospital outfits are green because it makes the patients more relaxed.

17

got a problem?

Dear Groovy Chick,
What should I do if I get a huge spot the day before the school disco?

Don't pick or squeeze spots — this can leave you with a nasty scar on your skin. Tea tree oil is very good for drying out pimples, so apply some before you go to bed. Next day you should be able to cover it with a little concealer.

Dear Groovy Chick,
My best friend is a fashion disaster. Sometimes she looks so bad people laugh at her. How can I help her get groovy?

Why not lend her some of your stuff to start with. When it's her birthday, buy her something cool to wear and, above all, make sure you leave this book where she can see it.

Dear Groovy Chick,
I have the curliest hair ever. It's totally out of control!
What can I do to stop it from being like a hay stack?

Curly hair is usually quite dry, so keeping it moisturised is the answer.
Always use a moisturising shampoo and conditioner when you wash it.
Smooth through a little anti-frizz serum while it's still wet and
leave it to dry naturally.

Dear Groovy Chick,
My mum goes mad if I wear make-up.
How can I get her to change her mind?

If you've got a party or disco to go to, ask if you can wear
some shimmer powder, lip gloss and a little mascara. Once
your mum realises you're not spending an hour
putting it all on, she'll probably lighten up a bit.

Dear Groovy Chick,
My mate hates shopping. She
never wants to come with me.
What will solve my problem?

Doesn't like shopping? Suggest you
go for an hour and stop for a drink
and a cake on the way home.

FASHION FACT

In Elizabethan England women thought that sleeping with slices of raw beef on their faces would get rid of wrinkles.

19

happy holidays!

SAFE SUN

Tans make us look and feel healthy,
but the sun is very dangerous.
Follow these rules to be safe in the sun.

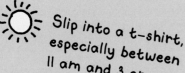 Slip into a t-shirt, especially between 11 am and 3 pm as the sun is very strong then.

 Slop on the sunscreen — spf 15 at least. Reapply every hour and after you've been in the water.

 Slap on a hat — keeping the sun off your head helps prevent you getting a nasty case of sunstroke.

Use lots of aftersun lotion to moisturise your skin after you've been in the sun.

 Make sure you drink plenty of water in hot weather.

20

HOLIDAY ESSENTIALS

You don't need to take a suitcase the size of a small country when you go on holiday. Use my handy checklist to make sure you have all you need.

Flip-flops

Beach bag

shampoo

Party sandals

2 pairs of shorts

2 swimsuits — wear them on alternate days

conditioner

Party purse or bag

shower gel

5 t-shirts

face wash

jewellery

2 sarongs

sun tan lotion

aftersun lotion

5 vest tops

hair clips and bobbles

sun hat

Travel in your jeans and trainers. That way you'll have them if the weather turns bad, but you won't have to pack them. Put anything you need for the journey into a handy backpack.

For going out at night, you don't need a complete outfit for each day. If you choose mix and match things you can easily make up lots of funky looks.

Try some of these combos –

Vest + jeans
Skirt + vest + cardi
Dress + cardi
Top + skirt
Top + jeans
Bikini top + jeans + cardi

Use accessories and different hairstyles to change your look each night.

FASHION FAC

22

Hot Holiday Hair

Keep things simple while you're on your hols. Check out my fab ideas for day and night.

Day

At the beach or pool, protect your hair from the sun by combing through a little conditioner. Now put into a neat ponytail.

For shopping or sightseeing don't forget your sunhat or a cool bandanna to keep the sun off your head.

Night

Funk up a ponytail with a sparkly bobble and some glitter hairspray.

Clip in some coloured hair extensions for a quick and easy way to change your style.

Sparkly hair spins or snappy beads make the simplest styles disco-tastic.

Brush through your bunches with bright hair mascara. You'll get funky colour that washes out easily.

Keep to the same simple styles as daytime, but add glitter and glam. Sweet!

23

sparkle and shine

Glitter is great! My glitter guide will help make sure you are a sparkly princess whatever the occasion.

Summer barbecue

Shine in the sun.

Smooth a little shimmer gel through your hair to catch the sunlight. Some highlighting cream on your cheeks will make you glow. Golden lip gloss looks lovely on sunny days.

Party

Look glam and gorgeous. Shimmery silver eye shadow and matching lip gloss looks great. A cute glitter tattoo on your upper arm or on your ankle will make you shine like a star.

Disco

You can be a glitter babe at night. Add some glitter on your cheeks and shoulders. Highlight your hair with sparkle gel. A crystal tattoo on your arm will catch the colours of the disco lights!

FASHION FACT

The first frosted make-up was made in ancient Egypt by mixing crushed ant eggs into face paints!

Don't try this at home

The Romans liked to take mud baths – in crocodile poo!

Ew!

Other gross ideas were mixing sheep fat and blood to make nail polish and using the blood of black cows for hair dye.

Yuk!

In ancient China and Japan it was the fashion to paint your face white with rice powder, pluck your eyebrows to almost nothing and then paint your teeth black or gold.
Lovely!

In the olden days, cosmetics were made from lead and mercury. This caused faces to become disfigured and sometimes even poisoned people to death!

shop till you drop!

Tips for top shopping.

Try to have an idea of what you're shopping for.

Buy items that co-ordinate with some things you already have. That way you can mix and match.

Never go shopping with boys. They will only hang around moaning they're bored.

The exceptions to the boy rule are dads. Dads will be so desperate to leave the shop they'll say you look great in everything!

Shopping with your mum can be handy. She'll probably lend you the extra cash you need for that to-die-for skirt.

FASHION FACT

Ouch!
In the olden days, women wore corsets laced so tightly that they could hardly breathe and often fainted.

Super shopping means lots of walking, so comfy footwear is an essential.

It's not a bargain unless you need it.

hair express

It's not hard to get glam hair. Pull your hair into a smooth, low ponytail to start then get set to change — fast!

Don't just use one band on your ponytail, put them all the way down.

Start to twist your ponytail from the neck to the end. Keep twisting and it will knot into a neat bun. Secure by winding a scrunchie round it.

Split your ponytail into 4 or 5 and braid each section. Fasten at the ends with bright hair bands.

Use a comb make a gap in your hair just above the pony band. Push the end of your ponytail through the gap and pull down to give a funky twist to your style.

Take narrow front sections and fasten them with clips all the way down. Now do your pony style.

Just add some cute slides or grips to the front of your hair. The shops are full of great styles.

FASHION FACT

Hair dying has been fashionable since ancient times. But the dyes were so harsh that lots of people ended up bald and had to wear wigs!

we love shopping!

My Top 10 reasons why we love to shop!

1. It's the SALES!

2. A girl can never have too many shoes.

3. You've absolutely nothing to wear.

4. It's a fab way to spend time with your mates.

5. Feeling dull? Get something sparkly.

6. A few new accessories can brighten up a tired old outfit.

30

fashion essentials

Going shopping? Not sure what to buy?
here are my lists for stylish buys...

tops:

gypsy top
black shirt
white shirt
plain jumper
embroidered cardi

other essentials:

dress
denim jacket
fitted jacket

shoes:

trainers
flat shoes
low heeled boots
party sandals
flip-flops

The things on these lists will all mix and match with each other.

32

You should be able to keep trying different mixes for ages.

Just buying a couple of new tops will give you a whole new look.

trousers:

smart
black trousers
cool combats
cropped trousers

jeans:

2 pairs of jeans –
one plain and
one party pair
with
beading
or
embroidery

bags:

backpack
denim bag
sparkly disco purse
funky shopper

FASHION FACT

In the early 1900s hobble skirts were all the rage. They got their name because they were so narrow below the knees women could hardly walk.

33

all change!

Different accessories worn with the same outfit can totally change the way it looks.

For a **sporty** look add trainers, backpack and a chunky chain belt.

FASHION FACT

In some American states it was illegal for women to wear trousers in schools, offices and restaurants until 1970!

Make it glam with a sparkly brooch on the jacket, a glittery necklace and boots with a small heel. A mini denim handbag and beaded belt will finish off the look.

34

You are wearing:
skirt + jumper

You are wearing:
dress + cardigan

 Go **cool** for school by adding tights and smart shoes, backpack and fitted jacket.

 To look **pretty** for visiting Granny wear tights and smart shoes with this.

 Get the **perfect** party outfit with shiny or sparkly tights and sandals. A sequinned choker and glitzy bracelet glam up your look.

 For a **smart** shopping style wear knee boots and a chunky coloured hip belt. Tie your hair into a smooth ponytail so that it doesn't get all messy when you're trying stuff on.

35

sort it out!

Now that you've got the basics, sort out your storage. You could be surprised at what you have at the back of the wardrobe. Here's how . . .

Keep similar things together in your wardrobe — have a section for shirts and tops, jeans and trousers, skirts and dresses and so on. Try to keep the same colours next to each other too.

Put anything that's freshly washed and ironed away immediately.

Dirty clothes should go straight into the laundry basket not thrown on the floor!

Sort out your shoes. Fruit boxes make great shoe storage. Hang your bags from a coat hanger. It's easy-peasy to find the one you need in no time at all.

Keep accessories in old shoe boxes. Label them clearly.

Organise your undies in the same way as your wardrobe — a section for socks, tights, pants and so on.

Get rid of all your unwanted clothes by having a swapping party with your mates. Hopefully you'll end up with some cool new stuff.

Anything left over that you'll never wear again can go to the charity shop.

star style

Wanna be a stylish star? Make sure everyone knows who you are by following these tips.

Wearing sunglasses gives you instant star style. Choose some with added sparkles for that superstar look.

Lots of stars love to change their hair colour. You can do it too by adding a clip in hair extension or braid.

Make sure your outfits are always perfect. Slobbing about in your baggy old joggers is not very star-like.

Every superstar wants to look their best.
But you have to work at it. Ouch!
Some groovy ways to keep in shape –

Shopping, shopping and more shopping –
all that walking is so good for you.

Slap on a CD, turn
up the sound and dance around your bedroom.

Roller skating
– don't forget your safety gear, there's nothing glam about scraped knees.

get skipping with your mates – fab, fun and funky

CD   CD

walk the dog

FASHION FACT

Film stars love their lippy. It was first made in the USA in 1915. Kiss-proof lipstick went on sale in 1925.

this old thing?

Make a denim jacket into something sweet by adding some furry fabric. Cut fabric patches and use invisible thread to sew them to the pockets, collar and cuffs.

Get a matching bag from the leg of some old jeans.

Cut off a section and turn it inside out. Sew across the cut edge to make the bag. Cut a long strip of denim for the strap, and then sew it to the bag.

40

I made it myself

Brighten up a cotton skirt with a funky tie-dye design. You'll need a pack of HAND dye, salt and some string. Twist and tie sections of the fabric using the string. Follow the instructions in the dye pack and get an adult to help. You'll have a fab new skirt in no time.

hand dye

salt

glue

You can buy sequins on a string from fabric shops and use for lots of different things. Stick them to the front of your dull flip-flops for twinkly toes.

Or glue them in diagonal stripes across the front of a plain vest top.

Ask an adult to help with the sewing, cutting, dyeing and glueing.

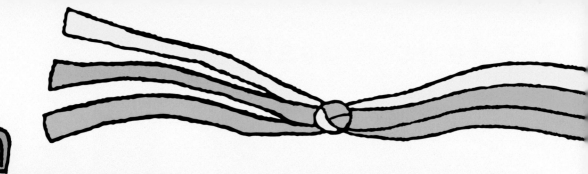

Make a pretty ribbon belt

All you have to do is get some long lengths of narrow ribbon in your fave colours. Knot them all together half way along the lengths. Tie more knots at even spaces from the first knot, but don't tie all the way to the ends. Now just tie round your hips in a bow and leave the ends hanging.

Use ribbon for a cute necklace.

Cut a length to fit round your neck and add your favourite pendant. Simple!

Want an exclusive design on your t-shirt that no one else will have? Make up your own arty design and copy it onto a t-shirt using fabric paints. Let it dry and follow the instructions for setting the colour – you may need an adult to help with this.

You can use iron-on transfers and patches to add sparkle and character to almost anything.
It only takes minutes, but ask an adult to help you with the iron.

from day

Oh dear. Spent too long at the shops and no time for a big change before that party? My day to disco tips will have you shining like a star in no time.

GET READY TO SPARKLE

44

to disco

SHOPPING
– jeans, trainers and crop top.

DISCO
– add beaded flip-flops, sparkly brooch to top, glitter or chain belt, shiny disco purse and glittery necklace.

SHOPPING
– denim skirt, plain shirt and trainers.

DISCO
– go prairie girl by adding ankle boots with small heels, a denim bag and woven belt.

45

SHOPPING
vest top, tracksuit and trainers.

DISCO
— get a bling-bling look by adding lots of glitzy pendants, a sparkly bracelet and shiny hoop earrings. Swap your trainers for cute flip-flops.

SHOPPING
bootleg trousers, plain gypsy top and boots.

DISCO
— for a sweet 'n' girly style swap your boots for sparkly party sandals, add a ribbon belt and choker and pick a tiny fringed bag.

disco hair

- try glitter slides
- add braids with ribbbons
- go for coloured hair extensions
- put on glitter hair mascara

shine on

Add shimmer powder or cream to cheeks and bare shoulders and choose shiny lip gloss for disco make-up.

funky twists!

Get a mate to help you do some funky twists — just put the hair into side bunches and start to twist each one. When they begin to coil round into little buns, pin them firmly with grips. Decorate with crystal hair spins.

47

Now you can be a fun loving girl too!

party quiz

perfect planning

get the look

groovy gift ideas

fun loving girl's
guide to parties

Now all your parties will be fun, fun, fun with this funky guide to being the host with the most and a super-popular party guest! Get into the swing of things with fab games and make it a 'do' to remember with the coolest party ideas!

ISBN 0-00-715222-1